ITALIAN HUMANITIES

ITALIAN
HUMANITIES

An
Inaugural Lecture

BY

RAFFAELLO PICCOLI, M.A.
Fellow of Magdalene College; Professor
of Italian in the University
of Cambridge

★

CAMBRIDGE
At The University Press
MCMXXIX

CAMBRIDGE
UNIVERSITY PRESS

University Printing House, Cambridge CB2 8BS, United Kingdom

Published in the United States of America by Cambridge University Press, New York

Cambridge University Press is part of the University of Cambridge.

It furthers the University's mission by disseminating knowledge in the pursuit of education, learning and research at the highest international levels of excellence.

www.cambridge.org
Information on this title: www.cambridge.org/9781107634435

© Cambridge University Press 1929

First published 1929
Re-issued 2014

A catalogue record for this publication is available from the British Library

ISBN 978-1-107-63443-5 Paperback

A N INAUGURAL LECTURE is an initia‑
tion ceremony, and some aspects of its once
sacred character are still inherent in it. I am
not trying to suggest that, contrary to the ac‑
cepted rule, it may be regarded as being more
of an ordeal for the lecturer than for the
audience; I am only hinting at the fact that
the rhetoric which governs at least its *exordium*
has the fixity of a ritual. But even in this
liminary part of my ordeal I must humbly
confess that I consider myself as sailing under
particularly auspicious stars, since in the per‑
formance of the customary rites I feel prompted
not by a mere sense of duty, but by the inner‑
most voice of my heart.

I shall not thank the late Vice‑Chancellor
and my Electors for calling me to this chair,
however greatly I prize the honour they have
done me, since I must thank them for a much

more generous benefit, that of bringing back to me the spirit of my youth which has for years been wandering among the cloisters and the gardens of Cambridge, and to which I know that I have not been unfaithful. Revisiting Cambridge after so many years, those truly spacious days of a time which now seems to be so fabulously remote, those studious, innocent, intelligent days, stand before me not as evanescent memories, but with the vividness that belongs only to our dearest dreams for the future. Small companies of friends assembled in a room at Trinity or walking up towards Madingley Hill or punting on the river near Grantchester, come back to me, not with these older faces we are wearing now, furrowed by age and experience, or with the ghostly visage of those among us who were fated never to return, and are now shadows in the asphodelian meadows, but still happy and eager in the immortal substance of their youth, in their intelligence, in their imagination, in their faith. Not a host of sad remembered faces, but a legion of living souls still advancing, perpetually advancing towards the goals they had set for themselves and for mankind in that miraculous halcyon time which preceded the storm: since the thought that flashes in the mind, the image that creates a new world in a sudden passionate illumination, the hope and the action which make this world a better place even for a fleeting instant, are everlasting essences though no book or human memory should record them, are the infinitely accruing treasure of merits which redeems our mortal race from the sins of its origin. Truly the dead are living, and their voices are not so feeble or distant that they may not still be heard; but why should those among us who have brought back from the storm, more or less withered or scarred or maimed, these perishable limbs, why should they have lost or renounced the imperishable part of themselves, their adoration of truth, their perception of beauty as of the inner meaning of life, their faith in the future of mankind? I am aware that I am talking in a

very simple and in what to many would ap-
pear to-day not only a defenceless but an inde-
fensible manner; I am conscious of the danger
of the clever smile and of the sceptic shrug;
there are generations now that have gained a
subtler knowledge through either an elegant or
a desperate disillusionment. I might easily dis-
guise my thought in a more fashionable language; but I prefer my words to be such that
the dead may recognise them. We have gone
through this horror and this desolation, and
our faith was not destroyed but strengthened
and purified.

But if my courage should ever fail me, it
would be enough for me to turn round and to
appeal for support from my predecessor in this
chair. I thank my stars again that the second
rite which I am expected to celebrate is not
a commemorative but a propitiatory one. It
would be presumptuous on my part to praise
the work of the first Professor of Italian in this
University. But Thomas Okey is one of those
rare men whose whole life is a clear parable

hinting at the concrete reality of the things invisible; and may his vigorous old age, since he
has chosen not to desert us, may it long remain
with us as a living testimonial of an unbroken
tradition, both English and Italian, of faithful-
ness to an ideal purpose and devotion to truth
and beauty. Okey's Italy is indeed a land
which has its existence rather in a platonic
or moral than in a natural geography of the
earth; it is the land of Dante and Mazzini,
sung by Meredith and engraved in Browning's
heart; that Italy which issuing from centuries
of decadence and servitude, and struggling
to establish her national unity and her political freedom, succeeded for the third time
in her secular history in becoming an ideal
model of universal validity for the rest of the
world.

I

If Thomas Okey was the first Professor of
Italian, the first official teacher of that language
and literature in our University was a young

man of whom enough already has been said, and who need not detain us any longer; unless I be allowed to remember a pardonable vanity of his which consisted in priding himself for teaching among the modern languages the one which had the most ancient tradition of studies in Cambridge. He would visit again and again the churchyard of St Mary-the-Less, musing on the pathetic inscription almost un-decipherable on the gravestone of an obscure Esquire-Bedell of over a century ago:

In Memory of

CHARLES ISOLA

Who died 28 Sept. 1814

Aged 40 Years.

Also 2 of his Children

And of

MARY his Wife.

Charles Isola was the father of many more chil-dren, one of whom was Charles Lamb's "silent brown girl," that Emma whom he fancifully believed to have come to him from an imaginary "Isola Bella in the Kingdom of Naples" (Ariel's island, I suppose), and of whom "S. T. C. acknowledged that she read a part of a passage of Milton better than he": an acknowledgment in which I used to find an indirect and subtle confirmation of certain ideas of mine on Milton's prosody. But contrary to what might have been legitimately suspected, I was not interested in Charles Isola's daughter so much as in his father, Agostino Isola, who styles himself "Teacher of the Italian Language" on the frontispiece of a collection of *Pieces Selected from the Italian Poets and Translated into English Verse by Some Gentlemen of the University*, which he edited in Cambridge in 1778 and again in 1784, and who in 1789 published what I take to be the only Cambridge edition of the *Orlando Furioso*, towards the printing of which the University contributed in 1787 the sum of fifty pounds. Agostino Isola is said to have counted among his pupils William Pitt, Thomas Gray and William Wordsworth. His name deserves not to be wholly forgotten, as it may stand for us as the symbol of a time when, the influence of living Italian thought and poetry being on the wane, Italian literature had almost come to take its place as the third of the classical literatures in the education of an English gentleman.

But as I left the churchyard of St Mary-the-Less, the grey and austere walls of Pembroke would bring back to my memory a still more ancient predecessor of mine of whom I know no trace beyond a phrase in a letter from Gabriel Harvey (sometime a Fellow of Pembroke, though at the time probably writing from Trinity Hall) to Edmund Spenser: a curiously tender and delicate phrase from the pen of such a vain, pedantic and irritable don: "a young Brother of myne (whom of playn John, our Italian Maister hath christened his Picciolo Giouannibattista)." It pleases me to fancy that in thus tenderly rechristening an English boy, our unknown Italian Maister may have been fondly caressing in his imagination the dear heads of his own children waiting perhaps for

his return in a little home by the shore of a
sunny sea; and I wonder whether we do not
owe to him the preservation in our University
Library of one of the most ancient grammars
of the Italian tongue, certainly the most ancient
that ever was written for the use of foreigners,
the *Regole della Lingua Thoscana* of the Italian
Protestant refugee Michael Angelo Florio, the
father of another young John, whose name is
now cherished by all lovers of Montaigne and
students of Shakespeare. The *Regole* are dedicated to "Signore Arrigo Herbert," son of
William Herbert first Earl of Pembroke: their
association with the Italian master of a man so
closely connected with Pembroke College is
therefore perhaps something more probable
than a mere surmise.

II

With Harvey and with Florio we are right
in the heart of the most significant period in the
history of the literary and moral relations between Italy and England, when it was the

dream of every young Englishman to acquire *le goust, et l'air de l'Italie*, following the already half-ironical advice of Monsieur Tornebus in the Latin epistle translated by Joachim du Bellay:

Doncques en Italie il te convient chercher
La source Cabaline, et le double Rocher,
Et l'arbre qui le front des Poëtes honore.

But let us attempt to retrace briefly the motives of this extraordinary and universal domination of Italy on the spiritual life of Europe during the Renaissance. Mediaeval Europe is, at least as regards the highest manifestations of her intellectual and religious life, a coherent supra-national unity: and this is true not only of her Latin and Catholic culture, but also of such vernacular expressions as Gothic architecture or French epic or Welsh romance, all of which become easily acclimatised in lands other than their land of origin, because they find a soil similar to that from which they have sprung. But at the dawn of modern times the differences in the historical backgrounds on which that common civilisation had grafted itself—like those seeds of which it is fabled that, having lain for centuries in the damp shadow of a sepulchre, suddenly they reveal to the world the grace and ornament of a forgotten spring—began to assert themselves in the rise of those distinct spiritual entities in which we recognise to-day the national characteristics of our several European countries. And Italy was the country where those fabulous seeds were more abundant, patiently waiting under the earth for the season of their flowering. Even now in Italy it may happen to you, as it happened to me on a sunny winter day a few months ago, to leave this world of light and colour, the rustic farm-yard where the children are playing with the goats, and to enter a subterranean world in the dark chambers of which the almost intact urns are being watched by exquisite images of rural and erotic deities, and are being slowly filled to the brim by a water purer and colder than that of any earthly fountain. If you are not deaf to the voice of such mysteries, you will then feel that those happy dead are germs of perpetual life sown by the hand of Providence, perpetually striving to emerge from the peace of their dark abode into the dancing light and the young scented winds of the world outside.

It was according to the natural order of things that Italy should be the first among the nations of Europe to produce a modern as distinct from and opposed to a mediaeval literature, and that it should fall to her lot to lay the foundations of the modern world. The Italian Renaissance does not consist in the rediscovery of some manuscripts and of some statues in the fifteenth century: it is coeval with the spiritual awakening of the Italian nation in the thirteenth century, and that rediscovery was but the consequence of the spontaneous birth of a new spirit. Dante remains at the confluence of the mediaeval and of the modern world, expressing in the universality of his poetry a vision too ample and too deep to be confined within either national or temporal determinations. But Petrarch and Boccaccio, and the rest of the

Italian poets and artists and scholars and thinkers between their time and the end of the sixteenth century, work for the creation of a complex image of the good life which is at the same time the integration of the classical ideal and the basis of modern civilisation. It is only in the sixteenth century, and under the guid⁄ance of Italy, that England and France and Spain emerge from the Middle Ages; Germany alone, though she had followed more closely perhaps than any other European nation on the steps of Italian Humanism, had to wait for a true Renaissance, delayed by the contrasting spirit of her religious Reformation, until the middle of the eighteenth century, the Sturm und Drang, and Goethe and Schiller and Herder.

Our Gabriel Harvey, since we choose not to abandon our Cambridge perspective, is caught, though not always unreluctantly, in the full stream of Italian influences in England. And, like the pedantic fool that he is, while he owes all his absurd ideas on classical English prosody to his Italian forerunners, and while he is constantly guilty of the worst Italianistic affectations, as when he addresses Spenser as *Liberalissimo Signor Immerito* or *Magnifico Signor Benevolo*; while his vanity is pleasantly tickled when, being presented to Queen Elizabeth on the eve of an intended political mission to Italy and France, the Queen remarks, in words which his own epic translation has preserved for posterity,

> bene factum, Jam jam habet ille
> Vultum Itali, faciemque hominis: vix esse
>   Britannum
> Crediderim potiusque hospes quidam esse
>   videtur;

while, in a word, he appears to us as being enough of an *Englese italianato* to answer the description of the *Diabolo incarnato* of another famous pedant of his days, yet he joins hands with the author of *The Scholemaster* in pouring contempt and ridicule on people he sees around himself suffering from the disease of which he is far from being immune. His *Speculum Tus-canismi*, written *in gratiam quorundam Illustrium*

Anglofrancitalorum, ought to be read together
with Roger Ascham's earnest warning against
the wiles of the new Circe. But these more or
less isolated voices in an England which, fash-
ioning her new poetry and her new national
destiny, was using the experience of Italy as
one of her most powerful tools, though quaint
and stridulous in themselves, are not without
a deeper meaning than appears at first sight.
The study of Italian influences in England
might in fact be easily employed as an acid test
for the recognition of the different spiritual types
and currents in her history. The England that
welcomed the teaching of Italy was the England
of Shakespeare, of Elizabeth, of the Cavalier;
the old England from whose face the traces of
Roman civilisation had never vanished entirely; a land vigorously human and terrestrial,
and yet full of imagination and of aerial mirth,
hard-working, hard-loving, hard-fighting. This
was the England of the Renaissance. But under
her brilliant and sensuous surface, far under the
luminous garland of clouds which curled

round her poetical and political Olympus, a newer and darker England was slowly maturing, looking beyond those clouds at the heavens above, and regarding life as an obscure pilgrimage towards a goal of indefectible light. Nowhere in Europe is the contrast of the Latin and the Germanic spirit, of Renaissance and Reformation, so dramatic and so significant as in England: until it finds a superior harmony in the solemn measures of Milton's song, where the Puritan ideal clothes itself in a Virgilian and Dantesque beauty, and a practical solution in the political wisdom and strength which allows both the Cavalier and the Puritan, those perennial and perennially contrasting types of the English mind, to work, to love, to fight side by side for the common glory of their country.

III

It would seem natural to think that Harvey's Italian Maister should not have remained without an uninterrupted lineage of successors down to our days. That period of Italian culture, from its inception to the end of the sixteenth century, which was present to the minds of Englishmen in the time of Elizabeth, is in fact not less important than either Greek or Latin culture for the full understanding of the history of poetry, of science and of manners in every nation of modern Europe, and in England in particular. If Italy, at the close of the sixteenth century, had been swept away from the face of the earth by a cataclysm, or if, like Greece, she had been conquered by the Turk, her authors from Dante and Petrarch to Machiavelli and Ariosto would now have a place in modern education similar to that of Homer and Herodotus, of Virgil and Tacitus. But there was at a certain moment a cleavage between Italy and the rest of Europe; and generally the intervening centuries are centuries of particularistic and secluded national growth. No spiritual unity was ever achieved in modern times comparable to the quiet domination of mediaeval univer⁄ salism, or to the irresistible impetus of Italian

Humanism. Italy continued to live and to think and to sing while her influence was slowly declining in the seventeenth and eigh-teenth centuries, flashing up again, but with a different spirit, for England at least, during the period from Shelley to Meredith. But her own actual life, her new original thought and poetry, seemed to be, in a sense, separated from the main currents of European thought. Her older literature had become a thing of the past without acquiring that prestige which, at least from an academic standpoint, inheres only in things utterly dead; and Europe lost the sense of the continuity of the Italian tradition, and is to this day but imperfectly aware of such im-portant spiritual events as Vico's philosophy and the poetry of Foscolo, Leopardi and Carducci.

There are fashions and revolutions in the world of studies as well as in the world of manners or of politics. I believe that Europe will have to come back to Italy, and therefore I have no doubts concerning the future of

Italian studies in this country and in this University. And not only on account of the importance of Italian poetry and art and thought in the past, but because modern Italian thought, from Vico to De Sanctis and Croce, is the only legitimate heir in our times of the great humanistic tradition of Europe, and its influence is bound to be felt in a Europe which is confronted by the same problems, aesthetic, moral and religious, which have beset the minds of these Italian thinkers.

Italian studies in English Universities have suffered from the disabilities common to all studies of modern languages and literatures, which were born too late to gain the full respect of academic opinion, and have had to make their way against a host of prejudices. But their position until lately has been particularly unfavourable, partly because when these studies were introduced into the Universities, other languages and literatures seemed to have a more immediate and actual interest, and partly because motives entirely foreign to the true aims of these studies, and of a purely economical character, were and sometimes still are allowed to dictate the choice between one language and another. I believe that from what has been said before, my hearers may easily infer what I consider to be the relative position of Italian, from an English point of view, in a complete *curriculum* of Modern Humanities. But Italian will never occupy in reality the position which is theoretically due to it, until the function of Modern Humanities is thoroughly understood and recognised in a general conception of the mission of the Universities in the modern world.

I shall come back to this point a little later. It is well that the ground should be cleared in advance of those whom I may call our brotherly enemies, the classical philologists. I am not thinking, either here or later, of conditions specially prevailing in this University: I am trying to deal with problems more or less present in the whole academic life of Europe and America. The classical philologist, having been born so many centuries before us, is in the habit of regarding us with the amused affection of the old for inexperienced youth and its inno⁄cent toys. And he has the advantage over us of a kind of esoterism which he owes to the fact that we deal in languages spoken to⁄day by the millions, while his languages are studied by the thousands and learnt, unfortunately, only by the hundreds. I can recollect, out of my per⁄sonal experience, the case of a classical master in one of the great English public schools, who would not permit a boy friend of mine to read an ode of Carducci otherwise than according to the quantitative scheme of similar odes in Latin and in Greek: this made havoc both of the poetry and of the language, as the most illiterate among living Italians could have told him. But with Virgil and Aeschylus they can do as they please; and they can indulge end⁄lessly in the game of conjectural readings, which anybody who has tried it on a modern author, even of his own language, knows to be falla⁄cious and dangerous indeed. They can bury themselves in the classics, and imagine that they can read them profitably without bringing to their understanding a mind thoroughly saturated with modern and contemporary thought. I am drawing a kind of caricature by way of mild retaliation; but no one will deny that this caricature does resemble more than one real face. Nobody is more conscious than I am of the importance of classical studies: and I cannot imagine a modern philologist who is not familiar with Greek and Latin culture. But it would do no harm if more classical scholars should learn from the example of such men as Sir James Frazer and Professor Murray that the only key to Antiquity is a deep knowledge and understanding of the spirit of yesterday and to-day. It seems rather futile to quarrel over the relative value of Classical and Modern Humanities, which are mere names of technical specialisations: both the classical and the modern philologist aim in reality at the same object, which is the deepening and strengthening of the historical consciousness of our

aesthetic, moral and religious civilisation. Both
the classical and the modern philologist were
suffering before the war from the dominance
of pseudo-scientific prejudices which Germany
had succeeded in imposing upon the whole
academic world at a time when her own
glorious philological tradition was already im-
poverished and corrupted. The linguist for
whom language was a mere natural pheno-
menon, and not the living expression of the
spirit of man, the critic who knew everything
about a poet but was too cautious to deal with
that unscientific entity, his poetry, are figures
of the past. A New Philology is being born
which is the legitimate offspring of the Human-
istic and of the Romantic Philology, and does
not consider anything human as alien to her;
which knows that her object is the history of
the spirit of man in all the forms of its activity,
and that philosophy is not the innocent Chinese
puzzle of professional metaphysicians, but the
substance and the flower of her own work.

Now if our Universities are not shaking

under the threat of the new Hun that wants them razed to the ground and the salt sown upon their ruins, it is partly, I think, because they are conscious of being, as it were, on the eve of this rebirth of Humanism. The world that has issued from the war may well seem to be in danger of losing that true perspective of human values which is the foundation of all art and of all morality, and which, in relation to Western civilisation, cannot be found anywhere but in a humanistic culture. In such a world our Universities, not as mere teaching machines, but in their intimate life as *universitates doctorum et studentium*, are, notwithstanding all their failings, centres of more intense spiritual awareness, through which only it is possible for this new and wider Humanism to counteract the mechanisation of the spirit and the tyranny of pseudo-scientific ideas by which our civilisation is threatened. The new schools of philology, if we take this to be the function of the Universities in the future, are destined to become within them the most sensitive organs of that historical consciousness of the spiritual growth of mankind, which lies at the back of all modern thought and of the religion of the modern world.

IV

But while we work with this distant ideal before our eyes, it is worth while to look around and take stock of the actual conditions of the Humanities in contemporary thought and feel-ing. If we consider the great currents of thought that swept Europe and America for a longer or shorter period, and sometimes as mere nine days' wonders, in recent years: Freudism, Re-lativism, Spenglerism, Behaviourism, etc., we find that they all originated not from human-istic but from scientific or pseudo-scientific sources. History and Philosophy, which are the only human science, have been deprived of this name by the mathematical and natural sciences. And the prestige of Science with a capital S is such that many among those who have dedicated their lives to the Humanities, are still asking themselves perplexedly every morning, whether such a thing as literature or history actually exists, and are not satisfied with their work unless they are childishly aping the mechanical and mathematical methods of the sciences.

This condition of things reflects not a purely intellectual but a deep religious crisis of the European spirit, and it is not without reason that it should be more apparent in Protestant than in Catholic countries. The close association of the Humanities with a religion entirely founded on revelation and on the authority of the Scriptures lasted in Protestant countries until yesterday. But the scientific discoveries of the nineteenth century were commonly regarded as dealing a severe blow to revelation and to the literal authority of the Sacred Books. Science appeared as the antagonist of religion, and therefore as the new religion, and the scepticism which it induced in respect of the Divine History ended by shaking all faith in human history also, and in the power of the human mind except when thinking, as people liked to say, scientifically. In Catholic coun' tries, on the other hand, the dissociation be' tween revelation and the Humanities began in the fifteenth century, if not earlier. The blow was dealt not by science, but by history, by philosophy and by concrete morality, that is, by the Humanities themselves; and therefore the triumph of science in the nineteenth cen' tury was infinitely less catastrophic. A human religion was already taking the place of the revealed one, and could be shaken but not destroyed by the victories of a thought which it recognised as its own child.

It is in this respect that Italian thought is beginning to influence and is bound to act still more vigorously and deeply on the spiritual conditions of Europe. We also ask ourselves what Poetry or Art is, what History or Science, what Philosophy or Morality; but we have answers to all our questions even though our answers have not that character of finality and conclusiveness which once was deemed necessary for the dignity of Philosophy. They are active, living, energetic answers out of which a wealth of new concrete problems perpetually springs, requiring new solutions and again positing new problems. The illusion of the discovery of an ultimate truth opens the inconceivable perspective of the death of the human spirit whose essential function is truth itself; but our thought, like every valid human thought, produces a *veritas filia temporis*, which has the character and movement, the dynamic dialectic, of life. We are deeply rooted in our humanity, and we call science only this direct and immediate, and yet clear and distinct, knowledge of the life of our spirit. Therefore we are interested in but not carried away by these wayward winds of doctrine emanating from the sciences, well knowing that nothing of any value for the creation of beauty, for the guidance of life, can ever come from them if not incidentally and, as it were, at a tangent.

The spectacle of an astronomer at his telescope, of a biologist at his dissecting table, fills me with the wonder and reverence with which I shall ever regard every form of disinterested human work. The spectacle of a scientific mind thinking within the self-imposed limits of his abstract or empirical method, has a beauty of its own which is only comparable with some of the most miraculous works of nature. But this admiration does not prevent me from seeing that science is not a theoretical but a practical activity, and that her abstract or empirical methods do not produce truths but instruments. While the character of what we may call, employing a very comprehensive term, moral truth, consists in the discovery of a thought which, as the Italian word goes, *invera*, or makes more true, all preceding and apparently contrasting definitions, a so-called new scientific truth supersedes and falsifies every previous theory, in the same way in which the invention of a new instrument or of a new machine compels you to discard the old one. The only indisputable progress which we owe to the enormous increase in scientific knowledge during the last two centuries, is the extension of the mechanical dominance of man over the forces of nature. But the more nature reveals to him the secrets of its structure, and the more his relative power increases, the less is man capable of maintaining his spiritual dominance, and of knowing himself not as a blind section of nature but as intelligence and consciousness.

The ways of nature which science presents to us are but a transcript for practical purposes of certain operations of the human mind on the dead body of nature; and as long as they are apprehended as such, they are a legitimate portion of our intellectual heritage. But the superstitious crowd, and some scientists who outside their special sciences are of the crowd, attempt to turn them into laws of our own human life. In a sense, however, the spirit of man itself is nature: it is the only part of nature which we know from within, with a knowledge infinitely more certain and intimate than any scientific theory. This knowledge tells us that even what we call nature as distinct from man, if we could apprehend it from within, if we could ever be-come the spirit of the tree and of the rock, would reveal itself as being all spirit and pur-pose, as striving with the same passionate im-pulse that we feel within ourselves, towards beauty, towards intelligence, towards con-sciousness. And therefore we are not going to accept, as the rule of our human life, laws which are imposed upon us as inscrutable and immuta'ble decrees of a blind deity, invested with an objective and irresistible authority, but which we know to be of human making, and destined to change in a few years unless, *quod Deus avertat*, some gigantic catastrophe should put a sudden stop to the progress of scientific thought in Europe and in America.

V

I shall end my words with this deprecation. But perhaps I may be allowed not to leave this chair to-day without a thought of gratitude and love for the University of Naples from which

I have returned among you, for the professors and students who were associated with my work, and I may say with my life, during the last seven years, and whose friendship and memory will endear that school for ever to me. For seven years the divine voices of Shakespeare and Milton, of Keats and Shelley, were listened to by us, by the teacher and by his classes, with infinite reverence, with ever renewed joy, establishing a kind of secret bond among those who were thus privileged to live in a sort of ideal England, in that enchanted island which contains the flower of the life of England during the laborious centuries of her history. Happy the lands that can build such monuments of immortal beauty out of the confused materials of this our mortal life! But happy indeed every land where man has left the visible or invisible traces of his struggles and victories, of his sorrows and joys, of his indomitable spirit, of his perpetual aspiration! I have stood on the hill at Cuma looking on the sea over which Aeneas steered his ship moaning for the fate of Palinurus, and on the long sweep of the desert shore where the Trojans burnt the body of Misenus, in his refulgent armour, over a pyre of cypress and oak. Nature, not unaided by man, has reasserted her empire over what once was the most venerable and ancient Italic town. Above the cavern of the Sybil, and all around the Greek platforms of the temples of Apollo and of Zeus, the vine and the olive-tree climb now the hill like young dancers, round upon round; and between the tender leaves of the vines and the pale foliage of the olive-trees, under which a wild profusion of flaming poppies is spread, the sea flashes in the morning sun with that azure metallic splendour which it certainly had when Aphrodite was born from its waves. Aeneas was the dream of a poet; but here Euboeans and Romans were born and worked and loved and fought and died; and the Christians came after them, and left the baptismal font in the cell of the temple of Zeus, and dug their graves in the hard stones of its platform.

Now all is but silence and light, *e più di lor non si ragiona.* Yet Nature herself, with her mystery and her beauty, crowns the ruins and seems to justify the ways of man to God.

All Saints' Day, 1929

Lightning Source UK Ltd.
Milton Keynes UK
UKHW022017290920
370746UK00005B/255